How Animals Care for Their Babies

by Roger B. Hirschland

NATIONAL
GEOGRAPHIC
SOCIETY

Washington, D.C.

Some animals, like these monkeys,
live together in large groups.
Grown-ups and older brothers
and sisters often share
the job of protecting
the babies.

Many creatures
make nests for their babies.

Maybe you have seen a robin's nest or a squirrel's nest. But there are many nests you can't see. They are hidden under the ground or inside trees. A European rabbit collects grass for her underground nest. The grass makes a soft bed for her babies.

The northern flicker, a woodpecker, makes its nest inside a tree. It uses its sharp bill to chip an entrance hole. Then it hollows out a nest.

Some animals lay eggs and care for them.

Animals may take care of their babies even before they hatch.
An anemone fish cleans its eggs with its mouth. A dusky salamander protects its eggs. This salamander lives on wet soil near streams.

A trumpeter swan sits on her eggs and keeps them warm. She gets up to turn them. This keeps the temperature even.

Some animal babies
are helpless—but others are not.

Newborn white-footed mice have
pink bodies with no fur. Their eyes
and ears are closed. They must depend
on their mother. She lifts the babies
gently to move them in the nest.

A mountain goat has a full coat of hair
at birth. It can see and hear. It even
follows its mother on steep slopes
just a few hours after it is born.

Most kinds of baby birds are fed by their parents. A baby flamingo stays warm under its mother's wing as it takes food from its father's bill.

Sometimes both parents find food for their babies.

Mountain bluebirds nest in old woodpecker holes or other hidden places. To feed the young, they catch insects all day long. When a parent returns to the nest, the babies open their mouths wide. The adult pokes the food down the babies' throats.

When both parents are together, you can tell them apart easily. The father's feathers are more blue.

Some animals nurse their young.

A mother baboon nurses her baby with milk from her body.
Have you ever seen very young puppies or kittens or hamsters?
Like all mammals, they drink their mothers' milk.

A female moose stands as she nurses her young.
The mother, called a cow moose, looks around for danger
while her twin babies drink. As the calves grow older, they
will eat leaves, twigs, and water plants, just as their parents do.
The moose is the largest kind of deer.

It's time for these brown bear cubs
to begin finding their own food.
They learn how by copying
their mother. They follow her
as she catches a fish and brings it
out of the river to eat.

Animals that live in groups often help each other.

A lioness licks the coat of one of her cubs. She helps it stay clean and healthy. Lions live in family groups called prides.

An adult baboon picks through the hair of a young baboon. Monkeys spend a lot of time grooming each other this way. It helps them feel close to the others in their group.

Sometimes animal parents need to move their babies.

Why do animals move their babies? A mother elk gently pushes her tired calf to cross a river. They may find food on the other side. Baby wolf spiders ride on their mother's body for safety as she hunts for insects to eat.

A lioness carries her cub to a new hiding place so enemies won't find it. She also takes it to where there is food.

Animals protect their young in different ways.

Fuzzy loon chicks can swim just hours after they hatch.
After a day, they can even dive, like their parents.
But during their first three weeks, chicks often ride
on their parents' backs. There they stay safe and warm.

A loon may flap its wings and rise up on the water
to frighten an enemy away from its babies. Loons live
on lakes, and nest along the shore. In the spring and
summer, they make loud, sad-sounding calls.

Some birds fool their enemies rather than fight them.

The killdeer lays its eggs on the open ground. Among pebbles or gravel, the speckled eggs are hard to see. What if a fox—or you—should come along?

Fluttering along the ground, the killdeer calls out and pretends its wing is broken. The fox—or you—will probably follow the bird and never see the eggs.

Parents stay near while their babies rest.

African elephant mothers help look after each other's young.
Sleepy babies take naps, carefully watched by the adults.
In arctic waters, white whales called belugas come to the surface
to breathe. A mother supports and protects her tired baby.

A young porcupine, which has sharp quills soon after birth, leaves its mother after eight weeks. Sooner or later, all baby animals grow up and make their way into the world.

Growing up is part of life.

When you consider how animals care for their young, you probably think about the kinds of animals you are most likely to see—in the wild, in a zoo, on a farm, or in your home.

Although many of the animals most familiar to children do feed and protect their young, the vast majority of species in the animal kingdom provide no such care. Most animals, including insects, amphibians, fish, and many kinds of shellfish, hatch from eggs. The offspring never see the adults that laid and fertilized the eggs. They face life on their own.

An animal that does not take care of its young is likely to lay hundreds or even thousands of eggs. Hatchlings are often larval forms that bear little resemblance to the adult.

Many children are familiar with some kinds of larval forms—the caterpillars of moths and butterflies, and the tadpoles of frogs and toads. Such young, without parental protection, face numerous dangers, largely from predators. Their survival rate is low. Yet, animals that provide no care usually produce high enough numbers to ensure the survival of at least a few of their young—and the continuation of the species.

The cecropia moth, or robin moth (pictured on the following page), is one such animal. The female, which may grow six inches long, lays eggs in rows and cements them to the surfaces of leaves. She never returns to the eggs. The caterpillars hatch in some 15 days, ready to care for themselves. They feed on leaves for a time, then spin cocoons, pass through the pupal stage, and emerge as adult robin moths.

Many of the moth's offspring will not survive. The caterpillars are preyed upon by birds, as are the pupae in their cocoons. Adult moths are often victims of predators, disease, severe weather, and impact with automobiles. But since one female may lay as many as 400 eggs, spread among numerous leaves, the chances are good that some of the offspring will survive until they themselves can reproduce.

Among the animals that do provide care, it is usually the mother, but sometimes the mother and father together, that nurture the offspring. A notable exception is the sea horse. Like the baby short-snouted sea horses in the photograph on this page, all young sea horses emerge live from the brood pouch of an adult *male*. At mating time, female sea horses deposit as many as 200 eggs in the brood pouch below the abdomen of the male. There, the eggs are fertilized. The male holds them in his pouch for about four weeks. As the young hatch, the male expels them into the water, and they are able to swim right away.

The capabilities animals possess immediately following birth or hatching vary considerably from species to species. The young of some animals, such as mice (8),* are totally dependent on their parents for food and for protection. Other kinds of young, such as fulvous tree ducklings (1) and mountain goat kids (9), require the protection and training of their parents, but are able shortly after birth to follow the adults and eat food on their own. And finally, some animals, such as the moth caterpillar, are completely independent of their parents.

Tiny sea horses emerge from the pouch on their father's belly. The female laid eggs in the male's pouch, and he incubated them.

Even within the same class of animals, the capabilities of the newborn may vary. Altricial birds are those which hatch featherless and sightless, and depend entirely on their parents' care. Familiar altricial birds include robins, blue jays, bluebirds (12–13), and many other songbirds. In contrast, the young of such birds as the trumpeter swan (7), the loon (22–23), many ducks, geese, and other fowl, including chickens, are precocial. They follow their parents

*Numbers in parentheses refer to pages in *How Animals Care for Their Babies*.